WILD·WORLD·OF·ANIMALS

OCEANS

MICHAEL CHINERY
ILLUSTRATED BY ERIC ROBSON

Kingfisher Books

Kingfisher Books, Grisewood & Dempsey Ltd,
Elsley House, 24–30 Great Titchfield Street,
London W1P 7AD

First published in 1991 by Kingfisher Books

BRITISH LIBRARY CATALOGUING-IN-PUBLICATION DATA
A catalogue record for this book is available from
the British Library

ISBN 0 86272 727 8

Series editor: Mike Halson
Series designer: Terry Woodley
Designer: Dave West Children's Books
Cover illustrations: John Butler

Phototypeset by Southern Positives and Negatives
(SPAN), Lingfield, Surrey.
Printed and bound by Cambus Litho Ltd, East Kilbride.

Contents

Life in the oceans

Thousands of different kinds of animals live in the oceans. Most of them live in the top 200 metres. Beneath this sunlit zone is the twilight zone. There is not much light here, but there are still plenty of fish and other creatures. Below 1000 metres, the sea is completely dark and very cold. Some very odd fish live here, mostly with big mouths and sharp teeth.

 OCEAN FACTS

● We take millions of tonnes of fish from the oceans every year, and many species are in danger of being wiped out forever.

 DO YOU KNOW

The deepest water is in the Marianas Trench in the Pacific Ocean. It is 11,000 metres deep, but some creatures even manage to live here in the cold and the darkness. Mount Everest could sit on the bottom of the trench without breaking the surface.

THE WORLD'S OCEANS

Oceans and seas cover three-quarters of the world's surface. They differ from lakes and rivers because they are all salt water. There are five oceans – the Pacific, the Atlantic, the Indian, the Arctic and the Southern – plus several smaller seas. Water temperatures vary from one area to another. The Arctic Ocean, around the North Pole, is largely frozen over all year round.

Drifting ocean life

The surface layers of the sea are full of plankton – small animals and plants that drift wherever the currents take them. Planktonic animals include tiny jellyfish, sea slugs and many shrimp-like creatures. The plants and animals of the plankton form a vital source of food, and without them there would be no other animals in the sea.

 DO YOU KNOW

The purple sea snail makes an unsinkable raft by trapping air in the slime from its foot. The slime hardens and looks like bubble plastic. The snail hangs from the raft and catches animals that bump into it.

The shrimp-like krill is only 5 cm long but it is the main food of the great blue whale and of many penguins.

Transparent, dart-like arrow worms, 3–10 cm long, attack other animals and kill them with sharp spines.

The sea gooseberry looks like a glass marble. It catches other animals with its long sticky tentacles.

 PLANKTON FACTS

● Sea urchins and many other animals live at the surface only when they are young.

● Plankton is most common in cold seas.

This weird creature will eventually turn into a sea urchin – if it is not eaten by one of the other animals.

The bony herring

The herring is one of the most common fish in the sea. It lives near the surface in huge shoals or schools which may contain millions of fish. Each fish watches its neighbours and they all swim in the same direction. They feed on small planktonic creatures. Herrings are eaten by bigger fish, and also by gulls and other seabirds. We catch herrings as well. They are very good to eat, although rather bony.

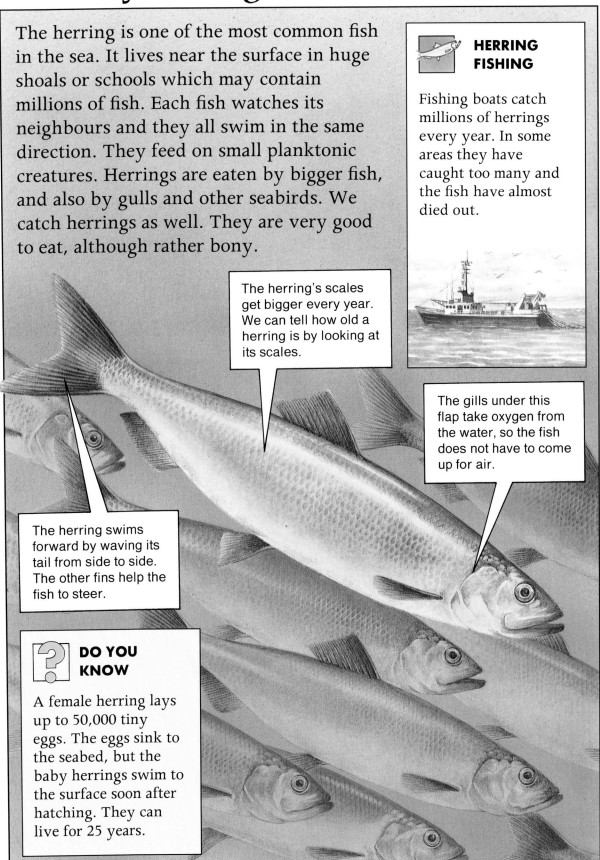

HERRING FISHING

Fishing boats catch millions of herrings every year. In some areas they have caught too many and the fish have almost died out.

The herring's scales get bigger every year. We can tell how old a herring is by looking at its scales.

The gills under this flap take oxygen from the water, so the fish does not have to come up for air.

The herring swims forward by waving its tail from side to side. The other fins help the fish to steer.

? DO YOU KNOW

A female herring lays up to 50,000 tiny eggs. The eggs sink to the seabed, but the baby herrings swim to the surface soon after hatching. They can live for 25 years.

The huge blue whale

The blue whale is the largest animal that has ever lived, but it feeds on tiny sea creatures only a few centimetres long. It takes huge gulps of water and then squirts the water out through the curtains of baleen that hang in its mouth. All the animals in the water are trapped by the curtains and then swallowed. The whale eats three or four tonnes of food every day. Blue whales live mainly in the Arctic and Southern oceans.

SURVIVAL WATCH

Early in the 1900s there were about half a million blue whales. But so many have been caught for their oil and meat that only a few hundred remain. Catching blue whales is now banned, so hopefully their numbers will increase again.

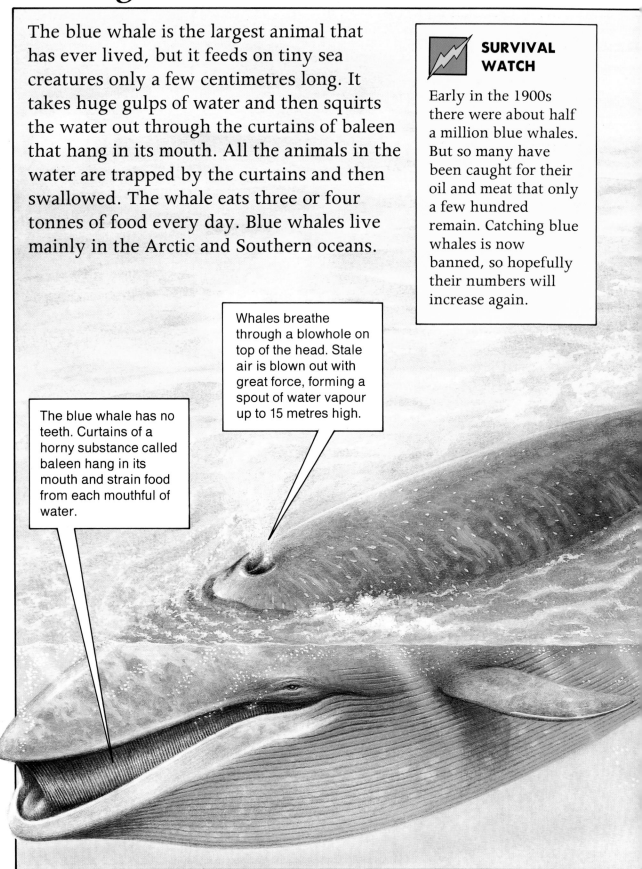

Whales breathe through a blowhole on top of the head. Stale air is blown out with great force, forming a spout of water vapour up to 15 metres high.

The blue whale has no teeth. Curtains of a horny substance called baleen hang in its mouth and strain food from each mouthful of water.

The tail is like a huge flipper, about 7 metres across. It beats up and down and drives the whale along at speeds of up to 30 km/h.

DO YOU KNOW

Whales are not fish. They are warm-blooded, air-breathing mammals. Their ancestors once had legs and lived on land.

Whales call to each other with sounds that travel many kilometres.

The baby is called a calf. Its mother pushes it to the surface as soon as it is born so that it can take its first breath of air.

BLUE WHALE FACTS

● The whale can hold its breath for over half an hour while diving.

● The blue whale may be over 30 metres long and it can weigh up to 135 tonnes – as much as 25 elephants or 1800 people.

Jellyfish

Jellyfish look like floating umbrellas. They have no brain and no skeleton. They swim jerkily by pumping water in and out of their bodies. Many have painful stings on their tentacles and use them to catch food, although not all jellyfish feed in this way. Some jellyfish are over 2 metres across.

This very common jellyfish, called Aurelia, is often washed up on the shore. Up to about 50 cm across, it is easily recognized by the four purplish rings on top. It can sting but it is not dangerous.

Four large frilly lips surround Aurelia's mouth, but the jellyfish has no teeth or any other hard parts in its body.

Aurelia has a sticky coat, which traps minute animals for food. The jellyfish licks them up with its lips, which then carry them up to its mouth.

A JELLYFISH GROWS UP

Jellyfish eggs do not grow straight into new jellyfish. The tiny creatures that hatch from the eggs settle on rocks or seaweeds and grow into what look like small sea anemones. These slowly divide until they look like piles of frilly saucers. Each 'saucer' then breaks free and floats away to become a new jellyfish.

The Portuguese man-o'-war

This strange-looking creature is a distant cousin of the jellyfish. It is really a colony of hundreds of little animals, all joined together under a sort of balloon that keeps them afloat. Each animal has its own job. Some catch food, others digest it, and others produce eggs. The man-o'-war's tentacles carry very painful and dangerous stings.

The sting of the Australian sea wasp jellyfish (above) can kill a person in just a few minutes.

The Portuguese man-o'-war got its name because it looked rather like an old Portuguese warship.

The bits that look like tubes are the mouths of the colony. They digest the food and send it round to all the other parts.

The tentacles are like fishing nets. A fish bumping into them is quickly stung to death and then pulled up to the man-o'-war's waiting mouths.

The tentacles can be over 10 metres long. They trail through the water as the main float is blown along by the wind.

Fish that fly

Several kinds of fish are called flying fish, although none can really fly. They just leap out of the water and glide along on their fins for a while before crashing back into the water. The largest of these fish is the devilfish shown here. It leaps high out of the water, but never glides very far. It falls back with a tremendous splash.

DEVILFISH FACTS

● The devilfish looks like a huge bat when it leaps from the water and it is sometimes called the sea bat. It is also known as the manta ray.

● The devilfish is not a dangerous fish – as long as it doesn't fall on your boat! It feeds on small planktonic animals as it flaps slowly along just below the surface.

The fins of the devilfish can be more than 6 metres across, and the fish can weigh up to 2000 kg.

The devilfish gets its name from the horn-like flaps on its head. The horns scoop food into its mouth.

SMALLER FLYING FISH

The smaller flying fish probably leap into the air as a fast way of avoiding their enemies.

Driven by its tail, the fish swims rapidly towards the surface with its fins held close to its sides.

Breaking the surface, the fish spreads its fins. A few more flicks of its tail and it is airborne.

Flights can last for over half a minute and carry the fish several hundred metres through the air.

The jet-propelled squid

The squid is one of the fastest animals in the sea. It sucks water into its body and then squirts it out through a narrow tube. The force of the jet shoots the squid through the water at up to 60 km/h. It can move both forwards and backwards. Squid eat fish and other animals, which they catch with their ten sucker-covered tentacles.

SQUID FACTS

● The giant squid is the largest of all the animals without back-bones. Including its two longest tentacles, it is about 15 metres long. Most squid are much smaller than this.

The squid can swim slowly by waving this fin at the rear of its body. The fin also acts as a stabiliser.

DO YOU KNOW

When a squid is frightened it squirts a cloud of ink into the water. Hidden behind this dark cloud, the squid can escape from its enemies.

The squid hunts by sight. It has excellent eyesight and its eyes are very much like those of humans.

The squid's tentacles are covered with suckers which hold the prey firmly while the squid bites it.

Sharks – terrors of the sea

Sharks include some of the most dangerous fish in the sea. Some of the bigger kinds, like the great white shark pictured here, are called man-eaters. They don't often attack swimmers, but if they do attack, their razor-sharp teeth can cause terrible injuries. Sharks normally eat other fish, although the huge whale shark feeds only on tiny plankton, just like the blue whale. Some of the smaller sharks are called dogfish. Most sharks give birth to active babies, but some lay eggs inside tough cases.

DO YOU KNOW

Sharks have no bones. Their skeletons are made of a soft material called cartilage.

Shark skins are covered with rough scales. Fishermen once used the skins to scrub ship decks.

Pilot fish often swim with sharks. People once thought they guided the sharks, but they are really waiting for the sharks to drop scraps of food.

A shark's tail is large and powerful. Side-to-side movements of the tail drive the shark forwards at speeds of up to 60 km/h.

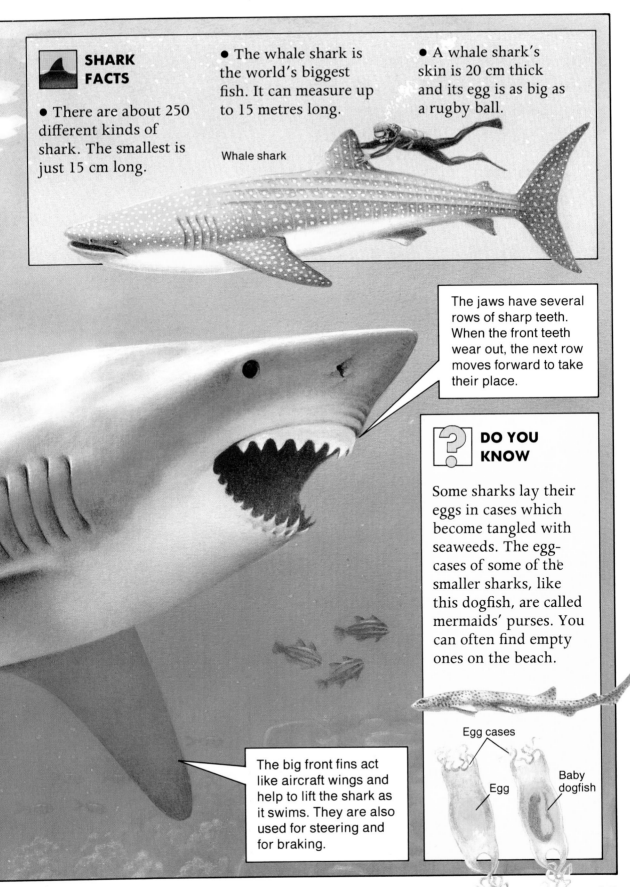

SHARK FACTS

- There are about 250 different kinds of shark. The smallest is just 15 cm long.

- The whale shark is the world's biggest fish. It can measure up to 15 metres long.

Whale shark

- A whale shark's skin is 20 cm thick and its egg is as big as a rugby ball.

The jaws have several rows of sharp teeth. When the front teeth wear out, the next row moves forward to take their place.

DO YOU KNOW

Some sharks lay their eggs in cases which become tangled with seaweeds. The egg-cases of some of the smaller sharks, like this dogfish, are called mermaids' purses. You can often find empty ones on the beach.

The big front fins act like aircraft wings and help to lift the shark as it swims. They are also used for steering and for braking.

Egg cases

Egg

Baby dogfish

The curious sawfish

The sawfish uses its strange snout to hit and wound other fish, and then snaps them up in its mouth. It also rakes small animals from the seabed with its snout. Sawfish live mainly in warm, shallow seas.

SAWFISH FACTS

- Sawfish can be over 7 metres long and weigh 2000 kg. The saw can measure over 1 metre.

- Sawfish look very dangerous, but they rarely attack people.

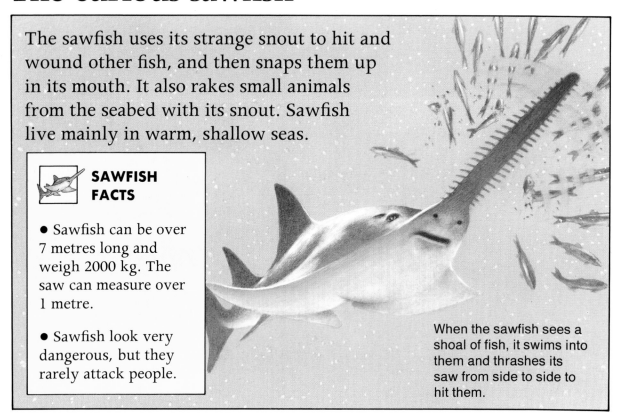

When the sawfish sees a shoal of fish, it swims into them and thrashes its saw from side to side to hit them.

The speedy swordfish

The swordfish is one of the fastest fish in the sea. It can reach 100 km/h in short bursts. It lives near the surface and uses its sword-like upper jaw to injure smaller fish.

With its streamlined body and powerful tail, the swordfish is ideally designed for swimming at speed.

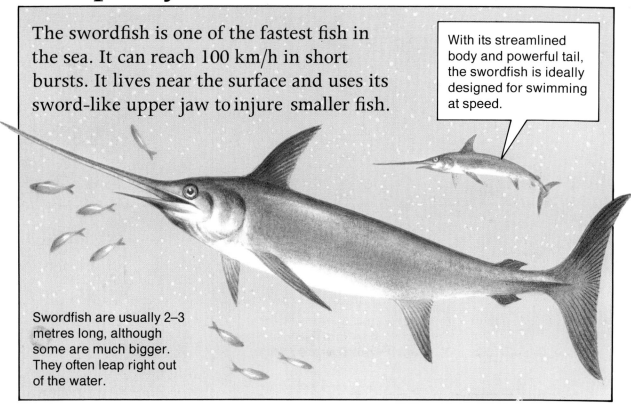

Swordfish are usually 2–3 metres long, although some are much bigger. They often leap right out of the water.

The cod – a fine food fish

Cod like cold water and live mainly in the northern seas, including the Arctic Ocean. They usually live in fairly shallow water and often swim close to the shore. The cod has a huge appetite and catches many other fish, including herrings. It also eats squid and crabs. Cod can reach lengths of 150 cm or more, but most of those caught by fishing boats are 30–100 cm long.

? DO YOU KNOW

Fishing boats catch millions of cod each year. The fish are caught in big nets or on long lines with thousands of hooks.

The cod is one of our most important food fish. It also gives us cod-liver oil, which is full of vitamins to keep us healthy.

Cod that live among seaweeds are brown or greenish to match their surroundings. Cod from open waters are grey.

Hundreds of short, pointed teeth help the cod to grab and hold on to very slippery prey, which is then swallowed whole.

COD FACTS

- A cod lays up to 5 million eggs, which float to the surface.

- The young fish sink to the bottom when they are about 4 cm long. They have many enemies and very few live to become adults.

Baby cod

Young cod

Intelligent dolphins

Dolphins are beautifully streamlined and spend all their lives in the water, but they are not fish. They are air-breathing mammals and are actually small cousins of the whales. They are very intelligent animals and scientists have recently learned that they talk to each other with a wide range of clicks, grunts, and whistles.

These bottle-nosed dolphins live in the Atlantic Ocean and the Mediterranean Sea. They can leap up to 10 metres out of the water.

 DO YOU KNOW

Dolphins are quick to learn and can be easily taught to do tricks in captivity. But many people think it is wrong to keep dolphins in this way and many are being returned to the sea. Bottle-nosed dolphins are the commonest ones in captivity.

The dolphin breathes through its blowhole when it comes to the surface. It also makes many different sounds through the blowhole while under the water.

The dolphin's tail beats up and down to drive it along through the water. Dolphins often leap high out of the water for the sheer fun of it.

Although they have small eyes, dolphins can actually see quite well. Even so, they rely mainly on their superb hearing to find their way about.

● The bottle-nosed dolphin always seems to be smiling, due to the shape of its head.

● The dolphin's peg-like teeth give a good grip on the fish and squid on which it feeds.

THE KILLER WHALE

The killer whale is really a large dolphin. Males reach lengths of about 9 metres. The animals hunt in packs and will often attack much bigger whales, although they prefer to eat seals, penguins, and fish. Even sharks are not safe from these powerful animals.

Like other dolphins, killer whales are kept in captivity and can be trained to perform various tricks.

19

The sperm whale – champion diver

Sperm whales are the world's best divers. They can stay underwater for two hours without coming up for air, and they go down more than 1000 metres. Males often visit the cold polar oceans, but females and young usually stay in warmer waters. They live in small groups called schools. The whale's huge head is full of oil, which helps the animal to float up easily after a dive.

SPERM WHALE FACTS

● Male sperm whales are up to 20 metres long. Females are much smaller.

● The whales talk to each other with loud clicking sounds.

The sperm whale has teeth only in its lower jaw. It feeds on soft-bodied squid, so it does not need to have big teeth.

SURVIVAL WATCH

Sperm whales used to be hunted for their flesh and oil, but hunting is now banned. This has made sperm whales fairly safe, but they sometimes get trapped in huge modern fishing nets. They die if they can't get to the surface to breathe.

Large squid put up a fight when they are attacked. Their sharp-edged suckers scratch the whale and leave scars all over its skin.

Big-mouthed gulper eels

The gulper eel looks like a terrible sea monster, but it is only a metre or two long. With its enormous mouth and elastic stomach, the gulper can swallow fish and other creatures bigger than itself. It lives in permanent darkness deep down in the sea.

? DO YOU KNOW

There is not much food deep in the sea. Fish down here don't get meals very often. Most have big mouths so they can swallow large prey, which will last them a long time.

Fish with headlights

The fish in the picture has a very unusual way of finding food in the sunless waters of the deep sea. It has its own headlights, which send out a beam of red light and so allow it to see other fish swimming in the surrounding water.

? DO YOU KNOW

Many deep-sea fish and squid carry lights. Some are used to find prey, but they more often help males and females to find each other in the dark.

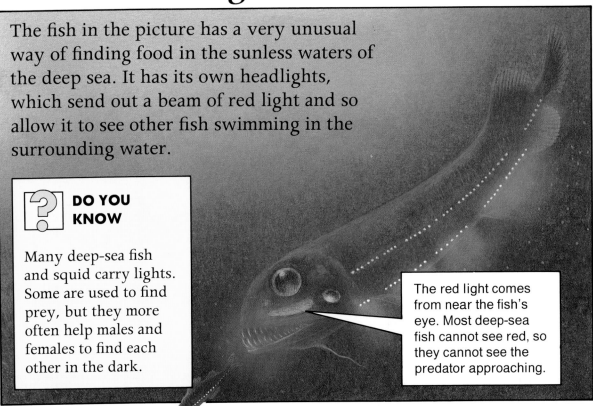

The red light comes from near the fish's eye. Most deep-sea fish cannot see red, so they cannot see the predator approaching.

The angler – a fish that goes fishing

The ugly angler fish pictured here live on the seabed around the coasts of Europe. They are up to 150 cm long. They don't move very much and they wait for food to come to them. The front part of the top fin forms a fishing rod, and a little flap of skin on the end of it acts as bait. Smaller fish which come to the bait are snapped up. There are many kinds of angler fish.

1. A small fish comes to investigate the bait waving about on the fishing rod above the angler's head.

2. The angler slowly lowers the bait towards its mouth and the small fish follows it down.

3. The angler opens its huge mouth and water rushes inside, carrying the helpless small fish with it.

DEEP-SEA ANGLERS

This strange-looking fish is one of many types of angling fish that live in total darkness deep in the ocean. This creature's shrimp-like bait has a red glow and attracts other fish right up to its mouth.

Lumbering lobsters

Lobsters are like very large shrimps. They belong to the large group of animals called crustaceans. They live in cool seas, usually close to the coast where the seabed is rocky. Lobsters feed at night on all kinds of living and dead animals, including other lobsters. Adults reach 75 cm in length, and weigh up to 4 kg. Their huge claws can easily cut through a person's finger.

SURVIVAL WATCH

Lobsters are a popular dish, and thousands of them are trapped each year. They are becoming rare and most countries now limit the numbers that can be caught.

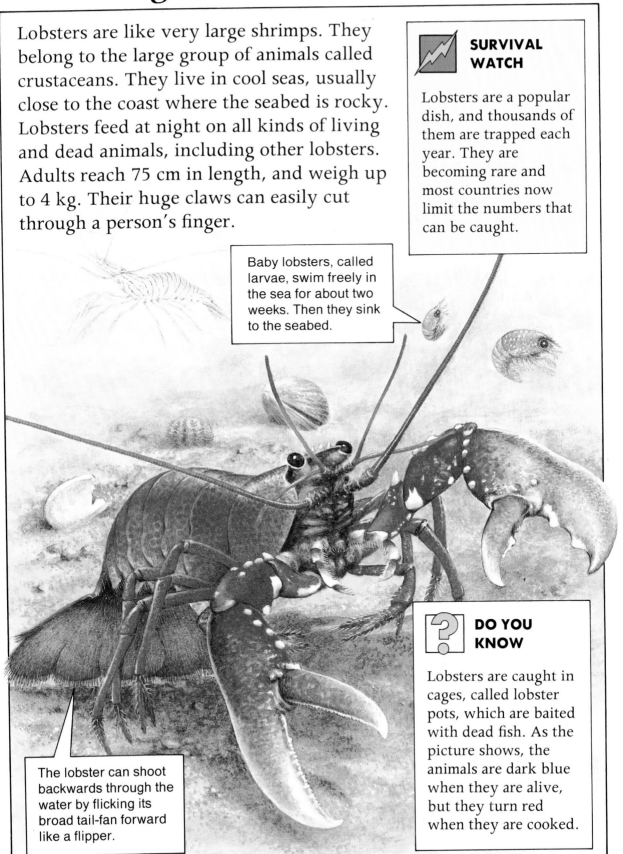

Baby lobsters, called larvae, swim freely in the sea for about two weeks. Then they sink to the seabed.

DO YOU KNOW

Lobsters are caught in cages, called lobster pots, which are baited with dead fish. As the picture shows, the animals are dark blue when they are alive, but they turn red when they are cooked.

The lobster can shoot backwards through the water by flicking its broad tail-fan forward like a flipper.

The octopus

Many people are terrified of octopuses, but these animals are not as dangerous as people think. Although some are over 6 metres across, most are very much smaller. They lurk among rocks and dart out to catch shrimps and other small creatures. They move by jet propulsion like the squid (see page 13), but can also crawl slowly on their eight arms. Octopuses are eaten by various large fish, which bite off their arms.

(see page 13)

SURVIVAL WATCH

Octopuses are very good to eat and they are becoming rare in some areas because people catch too many of them. Polluted sea water is also causing them to die out in many places.

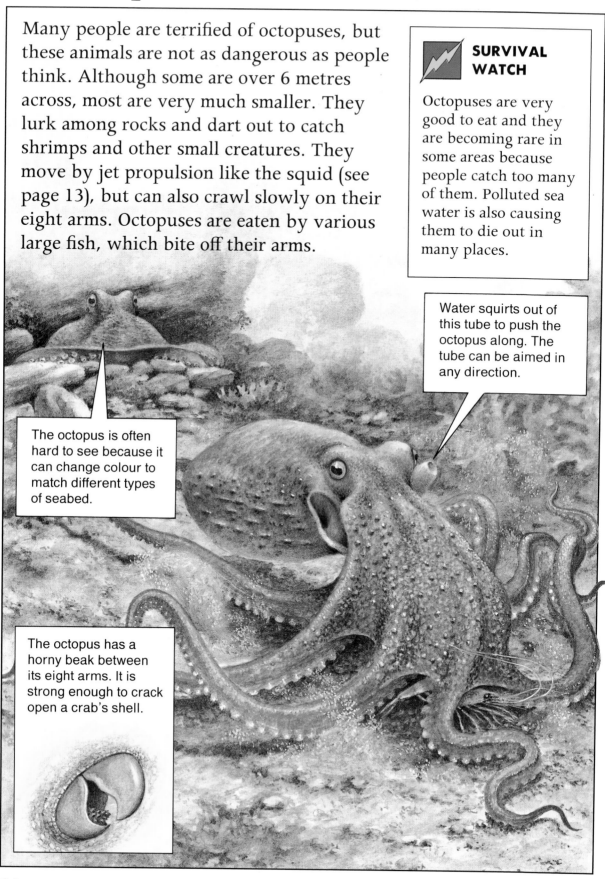

Water squirts out of this tube to push the octopus along. The tube can be aimed in any direction.

The octopus is often hard to see because it can change colour to match different types of seabed.

The octopus has a horny beak between its eight arms. It is strong enough to crack open a crab's shell.

Colour-changing cuttlefish

The cuttlefish is a distant cousin of the octopus, but it has ten arms like the squid. It can shoot quickly backwards by squirting water out through a kind of funnel. It can also shoot forwards to snatch a shrimp or other prey. Cuttlefish live on the seabed, mainly in shallow coastal waters. They are even better at changing colour than octopuses, and can alter their appearance completely in less than a second.

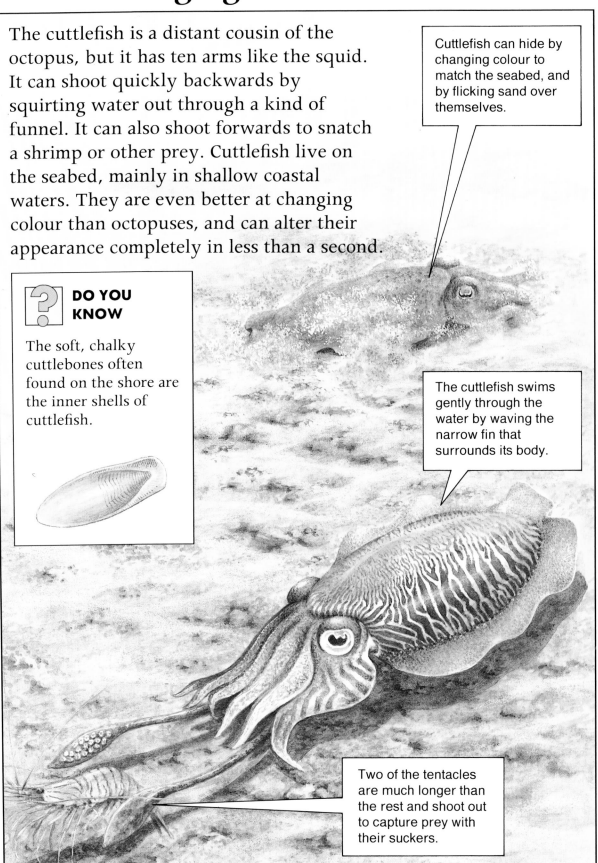

Cuttlefish can hide by changing colour to match the seabed, and by flicking sand over themselves.

? DO YOU KNOW

The soft, chalky cuttlebones often found on the shore are the inner shells of cuttlefish.

The cuttlefish swims gently through the water by waving the narrow fin that surrounds its body.

Two of the tentacles are much longer than the rest and shoot out to capture prey with their suckers.

The flat-bodied plaice

The plaice is a peculiar flat fish that lives on the seabed. Unlike the rays on the next page, it always lies on one side instead of on its belly. It almost always lies on its left side. It lives in coastal waters and feeds mainly on worms and thin-shelled shellfish. The plaice is a very important food fish and fishing boats catch thousands of tonnes every year. Most of the fish that are caught are about 25–40 cm long.

? DO YOU KNOW

A plaice can change colour to match various parts of the seabed. It looks at the surroundings and the colour cells in its skin then shrink or swell to change its appearance. The plaice makes the camouflage complete by flicking sand and gravel over itself.

Baby plaice

1. At first the young plaice looks just like a normal fish. It has one eye on each side of its body and swims in an upright position.

2. After a month, the skull becomes twisted and the left eye moves to the right side. The fish starts to swim on its left side.

3. The adult has both eyes on the right side, looking up into the water. Its body is covered with large orangey-red spots.

The torpedo ray – a shocking fish

Torpedo rays electrocute their prey by sending electric shocks through the water. The dazed prey is then easily caught. A big torpedo, up to 2 metres long, can give a person a very nasty electric shock.

The sting ray

The sting ray is a distant cousin of the torpedo ray. It gets its name for the poisonous spine on its long, whip-like tail. The fish lives mainly in shallow seas and feeds mostly on shellfish.

STING RAY FACTS

- The spine is used for defence. It is up to 35 cm long and causes painful injury if it is trodden on.

- Sting rays grow to 2.5 metres in length.

The coral reef

Coral reefs are like gardens under the sea. They are among the most colourful places on Earth but, unlike ordinary gardens, they are made up of animals instead of plants. The corals themselves are tiny animals and each one lives in a little chalky cup, which it builds itself. The cups cluster together to form the coral rock, and the living animals form a skin on the surface. Coral reefs are home to an amazing variety of fish and other animals.

The parrot fish eats coral. It snaps off pieces with its beak-like front teeth and crunches them up with its back teeth.

CORAL FACTS

● Corals are tiny relatives of the sea anemones.

● In the daytime the animals retreat into their cups and the coral looks like dead rock. At night they spread their tentacles to gather minute planktonic creatures.

Sponges are very simple animals which stay in one place. They feed by filtering tiny food particles from the sea water.

The sea anemone is a deadly trap for small fish and other animals. Its tentacles are covered all over with poisonous stings.

Reef-building corals live in clear, warm seas. The Great Barrier Reef, off the coast of Australia, is the largest of all reefs. Although built by animals the size of a pinhead, it forms a line of underwater hills 2000 km long.

Great Barrier Reef

AUSTRALIA

South Pacific Ocean

Southern Ocean

The conger is a large eel up to 3 metres long. It lurks between the corals and slithers out to catch fish in its strong, toothy jaws.

Angelfish are among the brightest of the coral reef fish. They are very thin and glide easily between the corals.

The crown of thorns is a large coral-eating starfish. It is rapidly destroying large areas of the Australian Great Barrier Reef.

The giant clam weighs up to 275 kg. Up to 1 metre across, it is one of the largest animals without backbones.

Cleaners and barbers

A few fish have found some really odd ways of getting their food. They have set themselves up as cleaners for larger fish. They are also known as barbers, and often have special places where they wait for their customers to come for cleaning. They clean wounds and remove and eat dead skin and parasites from the larger fish.

DO YOU KNOW

Fish that are searching for cleaners look for their bright colours. But some blennies and other fish imitate the cleaners' colours. When customers arrive for a clean-up, the fake cleaners bite them instead.

Cleaner wrasse

Blenny

There are many kinds of cleaners in the world's seas. They often have bold black stripes. This one is a cleaner wrasse.

Barbers and cleaners often work inside the mouths of larger fish without harm. This one is cleaning the mouth of a grouper fish.

The strange seahorse

Seahorses are among the world's oddest fish. They don't really look like fish at all, and get their name because the head looks a bit like a horse's head. They swim in an upright position, but spend much of their time anchored to seaweeds. Another odd thing about seahorses is that the female lays her eggs in a pouch on the male's body and leaves him to look after them.

There is a tiny mouth at the end of the snout and it snaps up minute shrimp-like creatures for food.

 DO YOU KNOW

Seahorses don't look as if they are real animals. Their bodies have many bony ridges and appear to have been made from wood or plastic.

The fin on the back beats rapidly to push the seahorse forward. The fish simply turns its head to change direction.

The male seahorse carries the eggs for four or five weeks and then gives birth to the babies. There may be 200 of them.

Seahorses anchor themselves to sea-weeds with their curly tails. They are often hard to see amongst the weeds.

Seals – super swimmers

Seals are sea mammals but, unlike whales, they can leave the water. They always come ashore to have their babies. The common seals shown here are members of a family called true seals. They are wonderful swimmers but rather clumsy on land. Eared seals are a different kind of seal and can move about more easily on the shore.

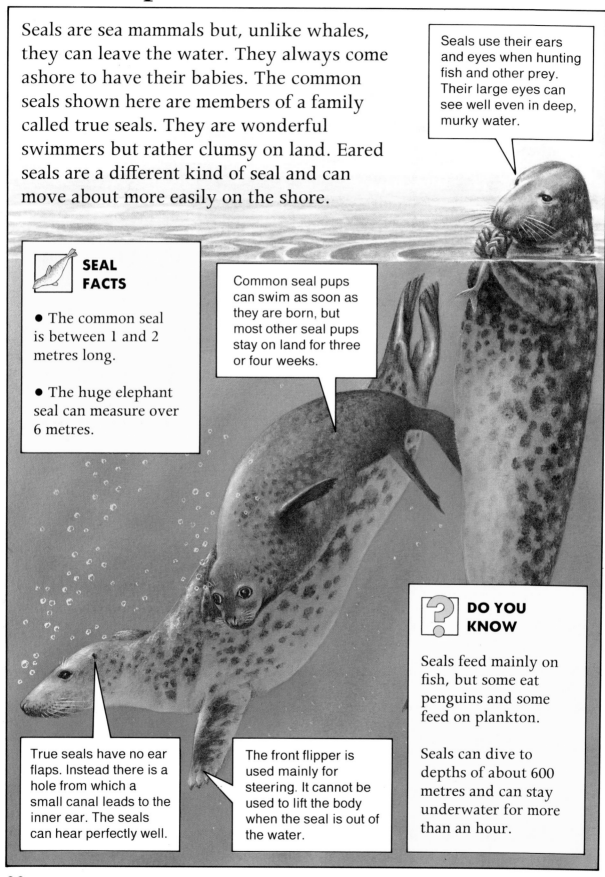

Seals use their ears and eyes when hunting fish and other prey. Their large eyes can see well even in deep, murky water.

SEAL FACTS

- The common seal is between 1 and 2 metres long.

- The huge elephant seal can measure over 6 metres.

Common seal pups can swim as soon as they are born, but most other seal pups stay on land for three or four weeks.

True seals have no ear flaps. Instead there is a hole from which a small canal leads to the inner ear. The seals can hear perfectly well.

The front flipper is used mainly for steering. It cannot be used to lift the body when the seal is out of the water.

DO YOU KNOW

Seals feed mainly on fish, but some eat penguins and some feed on plankton.

Seals can dive to depths of about 600 metres and can stay underwater for more than an hour.

Playful sea lions

Sea lions look like true seals, but they have ear flaps and bigger flippers. The front flippers can be used like legs and these animals are more agile on land than true seals. They live close to rocky coasts and spend a lot of time ashore. Males are much bigger than females. The sea lions shown here are Californian sea lions.

Sea lions have small ear flaps, but they can't hear any better than their relatives the true seals.

The back flippers can be turned forward and are used to push the sea lion along. They also do most of the steering when the animal is swimming.

In the water, the sea lion flaps its front flippers up and down like wings to drive it forwards at high speed. It feeds mainly on fish and squid.

SURVIVAL WATCH

Seals and sea lions have been hunted for centuries for their meat and their waterproof skins. Fishermen also kill seals to protect fish stocks. But seals and sea lions are still very common and few of the species are in any danger at present.

DO YOU KNOW

Sea lions have a wonderful sense of balance and can learn to perform amazing tricks. Many people think this is cruel, but the sea lions seem to enjoy it.

Dugongs – cows of the sea

The dugong is a really strange mammal. It spends all its life in the sea and looks rather like a seal, but it has no back legs. It is distantly related to cows and elephants and is the world's only vegetarian sea mammal. Dugongs live around the coasts of the Indian and South Pacific Oceans and graze on the meadows of seagrass that grow in the shallow waters. They are up to 4 metres long and weigh up to 900 kg.

DO YOU KNOW

The dugong probably started sailors' stories about beautiful mermaids. Floating with its head above the surface, it does look faintly human, but it is not pretty!

The mother dugong nurses her calf for nearly two years. The two animals float at the surface while the calf takes its mother's milk.

SURVIVAL WATCH

Dugongs have long been hunted for their meat and for the oil in their bodies – and also for the males' short tusks. They have been wiped out in many areas and could become completely extinct if hunting continues.

Dugongs are called sea cows because they graze the sea-grasses. They are also called sea pigs because they dig up roots and eat them.

Sea turtles

Turtles are sea-living tortoises. Their legs have become powerful flippers. The loggerhead turtle shown here lives in most of the warmer seas, including the Mediterranean. It eats seaweeds and all kinds of animals, such as prickly sea urchins and the deadly Portuguese man-o'-war jellyfish. It is unaffected by the poison.

 SURVIVAL WATCH

Some sea turtles are in danger of dying out because people collect and eat their eggs. Tourism is another danger. Turtles lay their eggs only on particular beaches, and if these beaches become crowded with holidaymakers the turtles will stay away.

Turtle shells are flatter and more streamlined than tortoise shells, making it easier for the animals to swim. The loggerhead's shell is up to 1 metre long.

The turtle's long front limbs flap up and down like the wings of a bird and drive the animal rapidly through the water.

Turtles spend almost all their lives at sea, but the females have to come ashore to lay their eggs. They usually lay them at night.

The female digs a hole with her back legs and lays over 100 eggs in it. She covers them with sand and goes back to the sea.

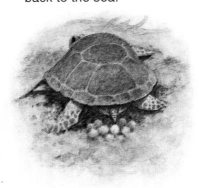

The eggs hatch in about nine weeks. The tiny turtles hurry down the beach, but many are caught by birds before reaching the water.

The restless albatross

Albatrosses are long-winged seabirds. They are as big as geese, but they glide and soar effortlessly over the waves for hours on end. They hardly ever flap their wings. Many albatrosses follow ships, and sailors often call them gooneys. Some birds stay out at sea for many years without ever coming to land, but they eventually come ashore to nest – usually in large colonies.

ALBATROSS FACTS

● The wandering albatross is the largest seabird. Its wings are nearly 4 metres across.

● Albatrosses pair up for life. Some pairs are known to have stayed together for over 30 years.

Long, narrow wings are ideal for soaring and gliding in the strong winds blowing over the open ocean.

The albatross uses its long beak to snatch fish and squid from the waves as it flies without actually having to land on the water.

DO YOU KNOW

Albatrosses nest on remote islands. The female lays one egg in a cup-shaped nest made with mud and grass. Some chicks are nine months old before they can fly. By then their parents are so exhausted, they need a year's rest before nesting again!

The frigate bird – ocean pirate

Frigate birds eat fish, but they don't always catch it themselves. They often chase other seabirds and make them give up any fish that they have caught. This is why they are called pirates. Frigate birds fly only over the warmer seas of the world.

A frigate bird chases a tropic bird until the smaller bird drops the fish. The frigate will then swoop down to catch the fish.

The graceful gannet

Gannets are superb divers. Flying about 30 metres above the sea, they dive at speeds of up to 160 km/h when they see fish in the water. A gannet's skull is very thick, to withstand the crash when it hits the water.

 SURVIVAL WATCH

Gannets nest on cliffs and small islands. Numbers have started to grow again now that people have stopped taking their eggs for food.

Bony plates covering the gannet's nostrils stop water from getting up the bird's nose when it dives at full speed into the sea.

Oceans in danger

The oceans are huge, but they are rapidly being polluted by the waste material we dump in them. Tiny bacteria turn much of the waste into food for plankton, but they can't deal with poisonous waste from our factories. Traces of poison are found in fish all over the world, and they are also found in seabirds – and people – who eat the poisoned fish. If we are not careful we will kill everything in the oceans and a lot of other animals as well.

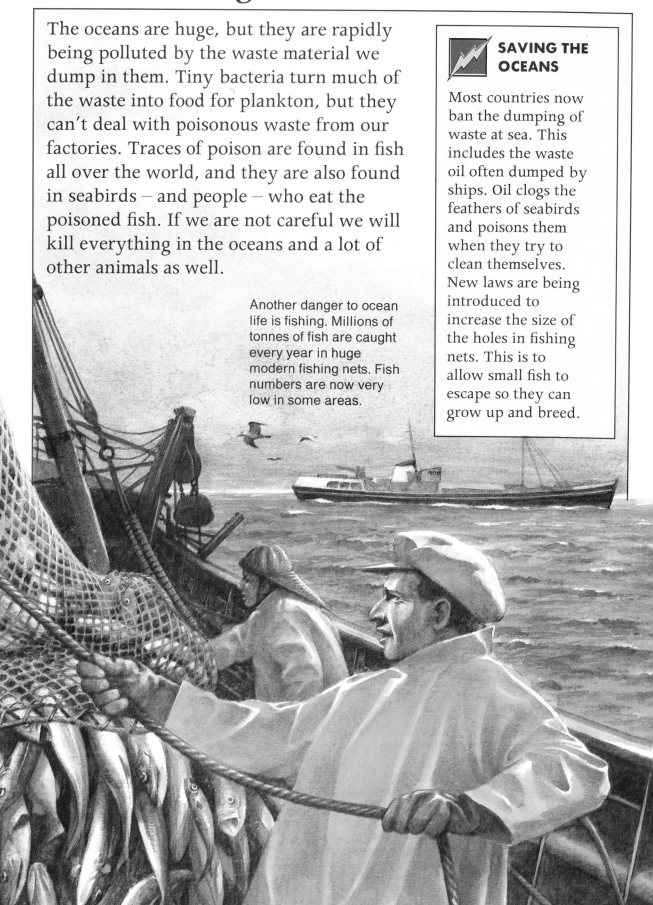

Another danger to ocean life is fishing. Millions of tonnes of fish are caught every year in huge modern fishing nets. Fish numbers are now very low in some areas.

Useful words

Baleen   The horny material forming the large curtain-like sheets that hang in the mouths of some whales and strain their food from the water. Baleen is also called whalebone.

Blowhole   The nose or nostril of a whale or a dolphin, situated right on the top of its head.

Camouflage   The way in which animals avoid the attention of their enemies by blending in with their surroundings. The animals are then hard to see. Many animals use special patterns or colours as camouflage. Others go one better and change their appearance as their surroundings change. Some animals also use camouflage to trap their prey.

Coast   The edge of the land, where it meets the sea.

Coastal   To do with the coast. Coastal waters are those close to the coast.

Crustacean   Any member of the lobster and crab group – hard-shelled animals with lots of legs.

Fin   Any of the limbs or other flaps which fish use for swimming. The fins are often very thin and delicate.

Flipper   Any of the paddle-shaped limbs of marine mammals and turtles. Seals use them for steering and for forward movement. Whales use their flippers just for steering and use their tails to drive them forward.

Mammal   Any member of the large group of animals which feed their babies with milk from the mother's body. Marine mammals include whales, seals and dugongs. Most mammals have hair or fur, although most whales are hairless. All mammals breathe air.

Marine   To do with the sea.

Parasite   An animal that lives on or in another kind of animal and takes food from it without giving anything in return.

Plankton   The floating mass of tiny plants and animals near the surface of the sea. The plankton is like a 'living soup' and without it there would be no life in the ocean.

Pollution   The poisoning of the ocean (or any other place) by oil or waste products from factories.

Predator   Any animal that hunts or traps other animals for food.

Prey   Any animal that is caught and eaten by a predator.

Shellfish   The name given to various hard-shelled sea creatures, especially cockles and mussels and their relatives. Crabs and other crustaceans are also commonly known as shellfish.

Shoal   The name commonly given to a large group of fish swimming together.

Tentacle   A soft, finger-like projection near the mouth of many animals such as squid, octopuses and jellyfish. Tentacles are normally used for catching food.

Vegetarian   An animal feeding only on plants.

Index